FASCINATING
HISTORY

by Bonnie Hinman

STORY
LIBRARY

www.12StoryLibrary.com

12-Story Library is an imprint of Bookstaves and Press Room Editions.

Produced for 12-Story Library by Red Line Editorial

Photographs ©: Harris & Ewing Collection/Library of Congress, cover, 1; Ammit Jack/Shutterstock Images, 4; LI1324 CC1.0, 5; Library of Congress, 6, 7, 20; A. Donnelly/Library of Congress, 8; Dario Lo Presti/Shutterstock Images, 10; George Stacy/Library of Congress, 11; J. Gurney & Son/Library of Congress, 12, 28; Brady's National Photographic Portrait Galleries/Library of Congress, 13; Frank and Frances Carpenter Collection/Library of Congress, 14; axz700/Shutterstock Images, 16; Kurz & Allison/Library of Congress, 17; T. B. Welch/Library of Congress, 18; wavebreakmedia/Shutterstock Images, 19; National Photo Company Collection/Library of Congress, 21; mTaira/Shutterstock Images, 22; Farm Security Administration/Office of War Information Black-and-White Negatives/Library of Congress, 23, 29; AP Images, 24, 25; Historic American Buildings Survey/Historic American Engineering Record/Historic American Landscapes Survey/Library of Congress, 26; Pavel Golovkin/AP Images, 27

Content Consultant: Dr. Jay Driskell, historian, visiting scholar at George Washington University

Library of Congress Cataloging-in-Publication Data
Names: Hinman, Bonnie, author.
Title: Fascinating history / by Bonnie Hinman.
Description: Mankato, MN : 12-Story Library, [2018] | Series: Unbelievable |
   Includes bibliographical references and index.
Identifiers: LCCN 2016046438 (print) | LCCN 2017000223 (ebook) | ISBN
   9781632354204 (hardcover : alkaline paper) | ISBN 9781632354907 (paperback
   : alkaline paper) | ISBN 9781621435426 (hosted e-book)
Subjects: LCSH: History--Anecdotes--Juvenile literature. | United
   States--History--Anecdotes--Juvenile literature. | Curiosities and
   wonders--Juvenile literature.
Classification: LCC D10 .H69 2018 (print) | LCC D10 (ebook) | DDC 904--dc23
LC record available at https://lccn.loc.gov/2016046438

Printed in the United States of America
022017

Access free, up-to-date content on this topic plus a full digital version of this book. Scan the QR code on page 31 or use your school's login at 12StoryLibrary.com.

Table of Contents

A Dust Veil Blots Out the Sun

The year 536 CE was a bad one for people across the globe. People in Europe, South America, and parts of Asia all witnessed something unusual. Early writers reported that the sun shone for only four hours each day. Some sort of dry fog or cloud of dust covered the sun. People did not know what caused it. They were unsure if the sky would ever clear.

The dust veil remained for almost two years. But its effects lasted much longer. The dust veil caused temperatures to drop around the world. Chinese writers recorded summer frosts and snow. Rain ceased, causing terrible droughts and food shortages. Famine killed as many as 80 percent of the people in some regions.

Scientists long thought a comet or meteorite had crashed into the earth and caused the dust veil. But recently, a researcher at the University of Texas at Austin discovered a more likely cause. Dr. Robert Dull found evidence that El Salvador's Lake Ilopango volcano erupted tremendously in

Did a volcano's ash block out the sun?

TREE RING DETECTIVES

Dr. Dull used tree ring evidence to learn about the volcano eruption. Scientists who study tree rings are called dendrochronologists. Trees typically grow one ring every year. Scientists use the rings to learn about the history of a tree's environment. Different colors and sizes of the rings can tell scientists what the weather was like.

approximately 535. The resulting ash and dust cloud could have caused the chaos in 536. Scientists say it could happen again. But the chances are only about 1 percent in the next 7,200 years.

18
Number of months the Ilopango volcano dust veil lasted.

- In 536 CE, a dust veil spread across the earth.
- The dust veil decreased temperatures and blocked the sun, causing drought and famine.
- Scientists think the eruption of the Lake Ilopango volcano in El Salvador likely caused the dust veil.

Lake Ilopango sits in the collapsed mouth of a volcano in El Salvador.

A Gun Misfire Saves President Jackson

On January 30, 1835, President Andrew Jackson attended a funeral. After the ceremony, a young man appeared in front of him. The young man fired a pistol at the president. He was less than 10 feet (3 m) away from Jackson.

There was a loud pop. But it was only the cap of the gun exploding. The cap did not light the powder as it should have. The gun had misfired. Jackson realized the danger. He rushed at the man, using his walking stick as a weapon. The would-be assassin pulled out a second pistol and fired. But it misfired, too. Jackson's aides wrestled the young man to the ground.

The man was identified as unemployed house painter Richard Lawrence. He said he wanted to kill the president because Jackson had kept Lawrence from being paid. He claimed Congress owed him money. Lawrence also told his questioners he believed he was King Richard III. He was later declared mentally ill. He spent the rest of his life in a mental hospital.

Lawrence's reasons for trying to kill Jackson were personal. But many

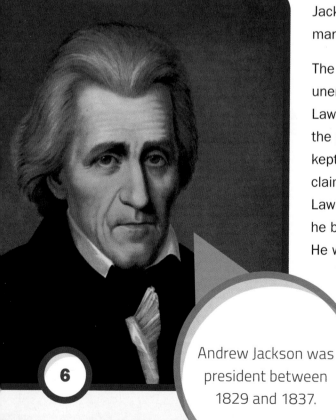

Andrew Jackson was president between 1829 and 1837.

Americans opposed Jackson on political grounds. President Jackson was a controversial politician. He banned the post office from delivering abolitionist pamphlets to Southerners. Abolitionists were people who worked to end slavery. In 1836, Jackson allowed the bill that created the central bank to expire. This was the bank that regulated currency between states. Without a central bank, states decided their own banking rules. If Lawrence had been successful, these things may not have occurred. The course of history may have been different.

12
Number of failed assassination attempts on US presidents and former presidents.

- Richard Lawrence fired two pistols at President Jackson.
- Lawrence spent the rest of his life in a mental hospital.
- The chance of both guns misfiring was estimated at 125,000 to one.

Southerners burn abolitionist papers at a South Carolina post office.

Henry Brown Mails Himself to Freedom

Henry Brown was born into slavery in 1816. He was enslaved at a tobacco plantation in Richmond, Virginia. In 1848, his wife and children were sold to another slaveholder. Brown's slaveholder told Brown to find another wife.

But Brown had a vision about becoming a free man. The vision told him to mail himself to a place without slavery. So he set about making the vision a reality. Two friends helped him with his plan. James Smith was a free black

An illustration of Henry "Box" Brown and his abolitionist supporters

250

Approximate distance, in miles (402 km), Brown traveled in his box.

- Brown's friends agreed to help him escape slavery.
- They shipped him in a wooden box to Philadelphia in 1849.
- Brown survived a rough 27-hour journey.

THIS SIDE UP!

Brown had written "this side up" on the box. He hoped this would help him remain upright during the journey. But despite this instruction, Brown and his box were handled roughly. He found himself upside down several times. The pressure from hanging upside down was intense. It made Brown's eyes feel like they might burst from their sockets.

Samuel Smith was a white shoemaker. Samuel Smith contacted the Philadelphia Anti-Slavery Society. He asked if the group would help Brown. The society agreed to receive Brown in the mail. Then, society members would help Brown get settled in Philadelphia.

Brown hired a local carpenter to build a wooden box. The box was 3 feet (0.9 m) long and 2 feet (0.6 m) wide. And at 2 feet 8 inches (0.8 m) deep, it was just large enough to hold Brown. The box had a hole in it so Brown could breathe. He planned to carry only a container of water with him. Metal straps and nails held the box together.

On March 23, 1849, Brown climbed into his small box. James Smith and Samuel Smith shipped Brown to Philadelphia. The journey would take 27 hours. Brown would travel by wagon, railroad, steamboat, and ferry.

Anti-Slavery Society members accepted Brown's box in Philadelphia. When they opened it, Brown said, "How do you do, Gentlemen?" Then he began to sing a psalm from the Bible. Brown was free at last. From that day, he was called Henry "Box" Brown.

The Mighty Maggot Saves Lives

Squirming, wiggly maggots disgust many people. Maggots are blowfly larvae. Female black blowflies lay their eggs in rotting flesh. A single blowfly lays approximately 250 eggs. Maggots hatch from the eggs within 24 hours. The maggots feed on the rotting flesh for a week. A week later, they transform into adult blowflies.

During the Civil War (1861–1865), doctors struggled to treat soldiers' battle wounds. If wounds did not heal quickly, infection occurred. Often, surgeons amputated arms and legs. Infection was less likely to set in with a clean cut.

Blowflies were attracted to soldiers' open wounds. At first, doctors tried to keep the flies away. But it was a losing battle. The flies swarmed the

Maggots make some people squirm, but they can help heal wounds.

stumps of arms and legs. A day later, the wounds were full of tiny, wiggling worms. It looked and felt disgusting.

This seemed to be a bad result. But then doctors noticed something they could not explain. Confederate soldiers recovered faster than Union soldiers. Doctors who treated Confederate soldiers usually had fewer supplies. They struggled to keep wounds clean. Confederate patients usually had more maggots in their wounds. The doctors thought these patients would be worse off.

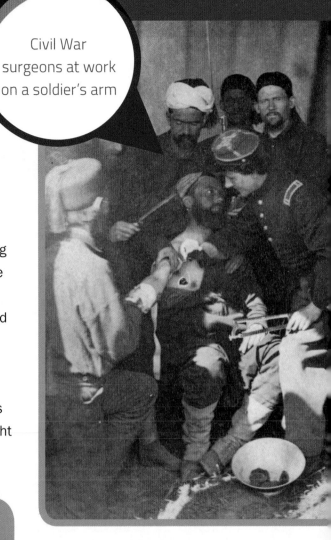

Civil War surgeons at work on a soldier's arm

60,000

Approximate number of amputation surgeries performed during the Civil War.

- Maggots are the larvae of the blowfly.
- Blowflies often swarmed the open wounds of injured Civil War soldiers.
- Maggots ate the rotting flesh, leaving healthy tissue behind.

But Confederate patients healed faster than Union soldiers did. They were also less likely to die from infection. A few doctors discovered the reason why. The maggots were eating the dead or infected tissue. The worms left healthy tissue behind. Today, doctors continue to use maggots to clean infected wounds.

5

An Older Brother Faces Tragedy

John Wilkes Booth assassinated President Abraham Lincoln on April 14, 1865. His terrible deed is taught in history books. But John Wilkes Booth had an older brother, Edwin. Edwin did not take the life of a Lincoln. He saved one.

Edwin Booth in costume as Shakespeare's Hamlet

John and Edwin Booth were both actors. But the two brothers did not get along. Edwin supported Lincoln and the Union side of the Civil War. John hated Lincoln. He supported the Confederacy.

John's murder of President Lincoln devastated his older brother. But one realization helped Edwin cope. He discovered he had performed a good deed months earlier. His actions had saved the life of Lincoln's oldest son.

Edwin Booth was waiting to board a train in Trenton, New Jersey. The station platform was crowded. There was a narrow space between the platform and the train car. The young man standing in front of Booth was accidentally pushed off the

100

Number of nights in a row Edwin Booth played Hamlet in New York City.

- John Wilkes Booth, younger brother of Edwin Booth, assassinated President Abraham Lincoln.
- Edwin was devastated by his brother's actions.
- Edwin discovered that he had saved the president's son from injury in an accident.

THINK ABOUT IT

Robert Lincoln felt he should have been able to help his father escape the assassination. Edwin Booth felt guilty for what his brother John had done. Do you think we are responsible for what our family members do? Why or why not?

The letter comforted Edwin Booth in the dark days after Lincoln's assassination. A Booth had killed a Lincoln in a horrible act. But another Booth had saved a Lincoln in a brave act.

platform. The man fell into that narrow space. His feet slipped into the gap, and he could not move. Edwin Booth grabbed the man's coat collar. He pulled the man to safety. The young man recognized Booth as a famous actor. He thanked Booth and continued on his trip.

Later, Edwin Booth found out the man he had saved was Lincoln's son Robert. Robert Lincoln told the story to a friend. This friend also knew Edwin Booth. The friend wrote to Booth. The letter told Booth he had saved the president's son.

Robert Lincoln was a young man when Booth saved his life.

13

A War Lasted Less Than an Hour

Most wars are at least days or weeks long. Sometimes they last for years. But the Anglo-Zanzibar War did not last years, months, or weeks. It began at 9:02 a.m. on August 27, 1896. It was over before 9:45 a.m. the same day.

Zanzibar is a group of small islands off the east coast of Africa. In 1896, the British Empire controlled Zanzibar. The British had a lot of influence over Zanzibar's government. The ruling sultan, Hamad bin Thuwaini, was loyal to

The Zanzibari palace was built on the Zanzibar harbor.

the British Empire. Thuwaini died suddenly on August 25, 1896. The British suspected somebody had poisoned him.

Thuwaini's cousin Khalid bin Barghash named himself the new sultan. He opposed British rule in Zanzibar. He formed an army to defend his new government. He and his men fortified the royal palace. They waited to see what the British would do.

The British officials stationed in Zanzibar told Khalid to leave the palace. Two British warships were already resting at anchor in the harbor. Officials called in three more. British forces numbered approximately 1,000 soldiers.

Sultan Khalid had nearly 3,000 soldiers but only a few ships. The sultan was counting on the British giving in. But leaving Zanzibar was not in Britain's plans.

At 8:00 a.m. on August 27, 1896, the British confronted Sultan Khalid bin Barghash. British forces again demanded he leave the palace. But Khalid refused to surrender.

4,100
Number of machine gun rounds fired by the British during the war.

- Zanzibar sultan Hamad bin Thuwaini died suddenly on August 25, 1896.
- Thuwaini's cousin seized control, but the ruling British demanded he leave.
- The British opened fire at 9:02 a.m. on August 27, 1896, and the war ended before 10:00 a.m.

The bombardment of the palace began at 9:02 a.m. The wooden structure quickly went up in flames. So did the royal yacht. Khalid escaped the palace through a back door. He left his soldiers and servants behind to fight.

The shelling stopped by 9:45 a.m. The sultan's flag was pulled down. More than 500 Zanzibari soldiers were killed or wounded. The British suffered only a single casualty. Khalid fled the country. A new, pro-British sultan took the throne of Zanzibar.

The Great Wall Is Not Tumbling Down

In June 1899, four bored newspaper reporters made up a story. It turned into one of the greatest newspaper hoaxes of all time. The four reporters worked for different newspapers in Denver, Colorado. They met one day by chance. The reporters complained that they did not have a decent story among them.

One of the reporters suggested that they make something up.

This was a common practice in the 1890s. Newspaper stories then did not always stick closely to the truth. Reporters would give readers something spectacular to read. This was called yellow journalism. True or false, these headlines and stories sold newspapers.

The Denver reporters came up with a story about the Great Wall of China. They wrote that the wall was about

The Great Wall of China became the target of yellow journalism in 1899.

7

Minimum number of papers across the United States that ran the Great Wall hoax story.

- Four Denver reporters decided to make up a good story for their papers.
- The stories reported an American businessman was on his way to China.
- The fake story was printed in newspapers across the United States.

YELLOW JOURNALISM

Yellow journalism started as a competition between publishers in New York City. The publishers competed to see who could sell more papers. Yellow journalism soon had a serious effect on US policy. The *Maine*, a US battleship, sank in Havana, Cuba, in 1898. Newspapers pounced. They called for war against the Spanish, who controlled Cuba. Doing so helped grow support for action against Spain. Later that year, the Spanish-American War began.

to be torn down. They said an American businessman was on his way to China. The fake businessman ran a demolition company. He was going to bid on the huge job.

The invented story appeared in the Denver papers on June 25, 1899. But other newspapers across the country picked up the story. Only the *New York Times* questioned whether the story was true. Readers soon lost interest. The Great Wall continues to stand.

Sensational coverage of the sinking of the *Maine* helped turn public opinion against Cuba.

Spelling Was Nearly Simplified

Founding Father Benjamin Franklin wanted to make English easier. He called for English spelling to be simplified. At the time, spelling was not standardized. Franklin proposed removing six letters from the alphabet: *c, j, q, w, x,* and *y.* He wanted to replace these letters with new ones he created. These included four new consonants and two new vowels. The changes did not catch on. But some scholars agreed with Franklin. They kept discussing his idea.

By the late 1900s, spelling attracted more attention. Some states passed spelling laws. The laws required schools to teach simplified spelling. Dictionaries began listing these simplified words.

In 1906, wealthy steel businessman Andrew Carnegie took up the simplified spelling cause. He believed simpler spelling would help more people learn English. He formed the Simplified Spelling Board. He donated to the board until his death.

The board printed a list of 300 words it wanted to simplify. The words would be spelled as they sounded. One was the word *you.* The board wanted to change its spelling to *yu.* It wanted to change *though* to *tho. Through* would become *thru.*

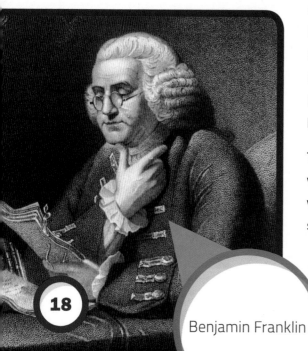

Benjamin Franklin

President Theodore Roosevelt thought simplified spelling was a smart idea. He ordered that all documents in his administration use the 300 simplified spellings. But Congress and the Supreme Court firmly refused. Roosevelt would continue to use the new spellings himself.

Simplified spelling did not catch on. But some of the simplified words are used today. It is common to see *thru* instead of *through* on signs and in texts.

Melvil Dewey invented the organizational system many libraries use today.

$25,000
Amount Andrew Carnegie donated to the Simplified Spelling Board per year.

- Benjamin Franklin wanted to simplify spelling.
- Businessman Andrew Carnegie formed and financed the Simplified Spelling Board.
- Theodore Roosevelt tried to require simplified spelling on official documents.

MELVIL DEWEY

Melvil Dewey was one of the founding members of the Simplified Spelling Board in 1906. Dewey created a library classification system. The Dewey Decimal system was first used in 1876. This system of organizing library books is still used in many public libraries today.

President Wilson Becomes the Shepherd in Chief

President Woodrow Wilson asked Congress to declare war on Germany in 1917. The United States entered World War I (1914–1918) on April 6. President Wilson understood that going to war would create hardship for American families. He wanted his own family to be a model for other Americans. He decided to raise sheep on the White House lawn.

President Wilson purchased a flock of 18 sheep. Its leader was an ornery ram named Old Ike. Old Ike liked to chew tobacco. He kept a sharp eye out for cigar butts left on the lawn. Old Ike was a good leader of his flock of ewes. But he did not like humans. Anybody entering his territory got head butted. This included the police who worked at the White House.

The backyard of the White House was perfect for grazing sheep. The sheep grew thick wool and produced dozens of lambs. They kept the grass trimmed and fertilized.

Woodrow Wilson

THE FIRST SHEEP

Sheep had lived on the White House lawn before Wilson became president. President Thomas Jefferson raised sheep. He brought a flock of sheep with him from his country home in 1807. He wanted to continue a breeding program he had started.

The sheep's grazing meant less work for groundskeepers. More men were free to join the military and fight in the war.

The sheep also raised money. Their wool was auctioned to the highest bidder. The wool raised more than $52,000 for charities.

By 1920, the war had been over for nearly two years. Wilson's flock numbered 48. The sheep had eaten most of the grass in the White House backyard. Wilson directed that the flock be moved to the front yard. There were many flowerbeds and small trees in front. Staff hurried to fence them off from the hungry sheep. When Wilson left office, he had the sheep shipped to a Maryland farm.

75

Number of sheep in the flock in 1927, when Old Ike died.

- President Wilson wanted to set a good example during World War I.
- He purchased a flock of 18 sheep to graze on the White House lawn.
- The sheep's wool raised more than $52,000 for charities.

Wilson kept sheep during the difficult years of World War I.

Project Seal Makes Waves for War

New Zealand and US scientists worked together during World War II (1939–1945). Project Seal began in early 1944 off the coast of New Zealand. The team developed a top-secret weapon. They hoped this new weapon would be as destructive as the atomic bomb. At the time, another team of scientists was working on that new weapon.

New Zealand provided most of the engineers to do the work. The United States provided the explosives.

The scientists experimented with underwater bombs. Approximately 3,700 bombs exploded in the tests. The team hoped these bombs would create tsunamis. These huge waves of ocean water could destroy a coastal Japanese city. The first tests were very successful.

Engineers discovered depth made a big difference in wave size. An explosion had to occur at just the right depth. If it varied even a little, the bomb produced a ripple.

A 2011 tsunami caused destruction in Japan.

The atomic bomb took priority over Project Seal.

This was far from the tsunami the scientists wanted.

To create a tsunami, the team had to explode 10 charges at once. The explosions needed to be set off approximately 5 miles (8 km) from shore. This would produce a wave of 32 to 39 feet (9.8 to 12 m). A tsunami of more than 30 feet (9.1 m) could devastate a coastal city.

4.4 million

Pounds (2,000,000 kg) of explosives scientists estimated it would take to create a 33-foot (10 m) tsunami.

- Project Seal began near New Zealand in 1944.
- The project's scientists used explosions to create large waves called tsunamis.
- Project Seal was successful but ended in early 1945.

But there was a problem. The scientists needed lots of explosives to produce one tsunami. A single tsunami was expensive to create. The US and New Zealand governments ended Project Seal in early 1945. The atomic bomb project became the top priority.

THINK ABOUT IT

The atomic bomb is called a doomsday weapon. It could create the end of civilization, or doomsday. Do you think doomsday weapons should ever be used? Why or why not?

The Weather Becomes a Weapon

Moving men and supplies was a big challenge during the Vietnam War (1954–1975). Much of Vietnam is jungle. In 1965, the roads were crude. During the rainy season, they became very muddy.

Muddy roads seemed like a big problem. But the US military saw an opportunity. They wanted to stop North Vietnamese soldiers from coming to South Vietnam. In 1967, the military began Operation Popeye. The mission: to change the weather. The military used a technique called cloud seeding. Airplanes flew over clouds and dropped a substance called silver iodide into them. Silver iodide particles caused ice crystals to form. The crystals fell downward

North Vietnamese soldiers used the Ho Chi Minh Trail to get to South Vietnam.

Muddy trails made travel difficult for US and Vietnamese troops alike.

and melted on the way. The melted ice hit the ground as rain.

Between 1967 and 1972, the US military performed more than 2,500 cloud seeding flights. Roads became impassable for up to 45 days after the rainy season ended. Operation Popeye extended the rainy season. But it did little to slow down the North Vietnamese supply lines. Muddy roads would have stopped vehicles. But many North Vietnamese soldiers carried supplies by foot.

THINK ABOUT IT

Do you think changing the weather is good, bad, or both? List the ways that it could be helpful. Then list the ways it could be harmful. Did making your lists change your mind?

9

Inches (23 cm) of rain produced in four hours by cloud seeding in 1967.

- In 1967, the US military began Operation Popeye.
- Planes flew over clouds and dropped silver iodide particles.
- Rain fell, extending the rainy season by as much as 45 days.

The Man Who Saved the World

Stanislav Petrov was a lieutenant colonel in the Soviet Air Defence Forces. On September 26, 1983, he was on duty in a secret bunker. The bunker was just outside Moscow, a city in the Soviet Union, now Russia. He had a very important and serious job. Petrov monitored the Soviet Union's early warning system for a nuclear attack.

At the time, the Soviet Union and the United States were at war. But there were no physical battles between the two nations. The Cold War (1947–1991) was a 45-year period of serious, hostile threats. Each nation threatened nuclear war against the other.

Petrov monitored a computer that received a signal from a satellite. The satellite was designed to detect nuclear missiles. If it detected a missile, the satellite would send a warning to Petrov's computer. Petrov would then alert his bosses. They would launch missiles toward the attacking country.

Just after midnight on September 26, Petrov's computer lit up. Its screen flashed, and alarm bells sounded. The computer said five missiles were cruising toward the Soviet Union. It looked as though they were coming from the

This missile silo was part of US defenses against Soviet nuclear attack.

United States. Petrov needed to call in the alert to his superiors. But he did not make the call. He thought it was a false alarm. He did not believe the alert system was reliable.

Petrov reported the alert to his bosses as a false alarm. He blamed it on a system malfunction. Then he waited to see if he was right. If he was wrong, the first explosions would happen in minutes. But no explosions came. Petrov was right. Life went on as usual for both the Soviets and Americans.

23

Number of minutes Petrov waited to see if the United States had actually fired nuclear missiles.

- Stanislav Petrov was on duty in a secret bunker outside Moscow on September 26, 1983.
- His computer indicated that nuclear missiles had been launched.
- Instead of sounding the alert, Petrov decided it was a false alarm, which it was.

Petrov, shown here in 2015, may have saved the world from mass destruction.

Fact Sheet

- Maggots have been used for wound care for thousands of years. The Civil War use was the first recorded use of maggots in the United States. Maggots were widely used through World War I and until the discovery of antibiotics such as penicillin in the 1930s and 1940s. Maggot treatment made a comeback in the 1980s. In 2004, the FDA approved maggots for widespread use.

- Operation Popeye was successful but raised some sticky questions later. The top-secret project was first revealed in 1971 by reporter Jack Anderson. As the details of the operation became public, many US leaders came out against any use of weather as a weapon. In 1976, many countries, including the United States, signed a treaty to stop any use of weather as a weapon. Weather modification research continues, but the results are to be used only for peaceful purposes.

- Stanislav Petrov was not rewarded for his good sense. He received a reprimand a few days later for mistakes in his logbook. Only years later, after the Soviet Union fell, were the brave actions of Petrov known. He received many international awards for his actions. Petrov said of the event, "That was my job, but they were lucky it was me on shift that night."

- Thomas Jefferson's sheep flock included a four-horned Shetland ram that was downright dangerous. In 1808, he knocked down a Revolutionary War veteran who had come to ask President Jefferson for a pension. Later, the ram killed a child. Jefferson had the ram put down in 1811.

Glossary

administration
The executive branch of a government, including the president and his or her staff.

amputated
Cut off all or part of a limb by surgery.

assassin
Someone who murders an important person in a surprise attack.

bid
To offer to perform a job for a certain price.

bombardment
An attack with bombs or shells, sometimes from ships.

famine
Shortage of food that leads to starvation.

hoax
An act intended to trick someone.

larvae
Young, wingless, worm-like grubs.

ornery
Irritable.

silver iodide
A yellow powder that can be used to create rain.

sultan
The ruler of a Muslim country.

For More Information

Books

Bearce, Stephanie. *The Cold War: Secrets, Special Missions, and Hidden Facts about the CIA, KGB, and MI6.* Waco, TX: Prufrock, 2015.

Demuth, Patricia Brennan. *Where Is the Great Wall?* New York: Grosset & Dunlap, 2015.

Frith, Margaret. *Who Was Woodrow Wilson?* New York: Grosset & Dunlap, 2015.

Visit 12StoryLibrary.com

Scan the code or use your school's login at **12StoryLibrary.com** for recent updates about this topic and a full digital version of this book. Enjoy free access to:

- Digital ebook
- Breaking news updates
- Live content feeds
- Videos, interactive maps, and graphics
- Additional web resources

Note to educators: Visit 12StoryLibrary.com/register to sign up for free premium website access. Enjoy live content plus a full digital version of every 12-Story Library book you own for every student at your school.

Index

About the Author

Bonnie Hinman has written more than
45 books, most of them nonfiction.
Hinman lives with her husband, Bill, in
southwest Missouri near her children
and grandchildren.